T0001551

101 WAYS TO BE AN ECO-HERO

KAIT EATON

CONTENTS

YOUR MISSION STARTS HERE!

The Earth is in crisis and we need to work together to help it. If we want to save the rainforest, allow endangered species to thrive, and stop the weather from becoming more extreme, we all need to start making changes to the way we live our lives.

DO YOU WANT TO HELP WHIP THE PLANET INTO SHAPE?

We could all learn to treat Earth with a little more kindness and pave the way for future generations. Thankfully, there are plenty of ways you can do jus that, and they start small!

Each person and every household has an impact on bigger things: from climate change to habitat loss. So with your help, we humans can play a huge par in an eco-revolution!

My name's Rhino Ray and I'll be traveling with you on you planet-saving journey. Look for my "Be a Hero!" and! "Stay Super!" tips for advic on how to become an ultim eco-hero—just like me!

STOP THE PRESSES! BURPS AND FARTS ARE DAMAGING OUR EARTH'S ATMOSPHERE! COWS RELEASE A HARMFUL GREENHOUSE GAS CALLED METHANE EVERY TIME THEY PASS WIND, WHICH IS CONTRIBUTING SIGNIFICANTLY TO CLIMATE CHANGE. THERE ARE OVER 1 BILLION COWS WORLDWIDE, SO THAT'S A LOT OF NASTY GAS FLOATING ABOUT...

YOU ARE NOT ALONE

Don't worry—the eco-hero mission is not only down to you. There are countless people just like you trying to make a difference, and you can join like-minded individuals in the quest to save our planet in local community projects, school initiatives, and international organizations.

GET YOUR GROWN-UPS INVOLVED

There are lots of tips inside that will require adult guidance, so make sure to reach out to parents and guardians for a helping hand.

GO FOR IT!

Just picking up this book is the first step to kick-starting your eco-journey and helping spread the word to those around you. The following chapters are made up of different themes, but you can start reading anywhere. And as you'll soon find out, there are countless ways to make a difference! So, what are you waiting for? Let's do this!

WS FLASH! RAINFORESTS ARE SHRINKING AT A RATE OF 30 SOCCER FIELDS EVERY MINUTE! IF WE DON'T ACT NOW, MANY TROPICAL ECIES WILL BE LOST FOREVER, AND THE BALANCE REQUIRED FOR LIFE ON EARTH TO FLOURISH WILL BE SPOILED...

Have a go at growing your own fruit, vegetables, and herbs. There's something to be grown in even the smallest of spaces!

SAVING THE PLANET BEGINS AT HOME

Superheroes start small but aim big.
You can do wonders from your very own
doorstep: recycle, upcycle, get green-fingered,
or try a digital detox. Where will your journey
to becoming a true eco-hero begin?

GLUE

FIND YOUR INNER ECO-HERO

**We can all be eco-heroes.
We just might need to change some habits first...**

1 CHECK YOUR CARBON FOOTPRINT

Your carbon footprint (also known as environmental footprint) is the amount of carbon dioxide released into the atmosphere as a result of the things you do. The idea is to make it as small as possible, so less nasty stuff gets pumped into the air. Take this quiz to see how big or small your carbon footprint is, and how close you are to becoming a fully fledged eco-hero.

1. Do you usually take a shower or a bath?
A) A quick shower is all it takes!
B) Depends on how I'm feeling...
C) Mostly baths. I just love to wallow
—the deeper, the better!

2. Do you and your family recycle?
A) Yes, we recycle everything
B) Sometimes, but only when we remember to
C) Not really, most things go in the household trash bin

3. How do you usually get to school?
A) I walk, cycle, or scoot / I am home-schooled
B) We carpool / I go on the bus
C) We go in the car

4. How often do you eat fast food or get takeout?
A) Rarely or never
B) Occasionally, as a treat
C) Most days

5. How often do you eat meat?
A) Never—I'm pescatarian, vegetarian, or vegan
B) I eat a mixture of meat and veggie meals
C) Most of my meals contain meat—I am a true carnivore!

6. Do you and your family own a composting bin?
A) Yes—we use it all the time!
B) Yes, but we don't use it much
C) Nope

7. How much screen time do you have each day (e.g., watching TV, using the computer for school work, playing video games)? Be honest!

A) Less than two hours
B) Two to four hours
C) Over four hours

8. Do you turn switches off when you leave the room?

A) Yes, always
B) Sometimes—usually when someone reminds me
C) No. I know I should, but I always forget!

9. How often is your heating on?

A) Rarely—usually if we can't warm up by putting on an extra sweater!
B) Every day in the winter, and we occasionally put it on at other times
C) We like our house toasty, so it's pretty much on all the time...

10. What's in your packed lunch?

A) Home-prepared food in reusable containers and a refillable water bottle
B) Mostly home-prepared food plus one or two pre-packaged items
C) Mostly pre-packaged food and drink

MOSTLY A's
Wow! You really are doing all you can to protect the planet and save it for future generations. Your carbon footprint is already smaller than average and you are well on your way to becoming an eco-hero. Now you just need to help spread the word!

MOSTLY B's
Well, you are definitely on the right track. Just make a few simple changes to reduce your carbon footprint, and you'll be able to wear your eco-hero cape with pride. You can do this!

MOSTLY C's
Your carbon footprint is pretty big, but all hope is not lost! By making some small changes to your habits, you can make sure that your inner eco-hero will emerge victorious. Read on to pick up some tips!

STOP WASTE!

Making these small changes every day will make a BIG difference over your lifetime!

2 SHOWER INSTEAD OF BATH

It's simple—a shower uses less water than a bath, so making this change is a really easy way to help the environment. And a quick shower is even better (although make it long enough to ensure you are clean)! Why not time yourself, then challenge the rest of your family to see if they can beat you?

3 TURN OFF LIGHTS AND ELECTRONICS

The majority of the electricity we use is created by burning fossil fuels, such as coal and gas. But burning these fossil fuels creates greenhouse gases, which in turn contributes to global warming. So every time you turn off lights or electronics, fewer pollutants are entering our atmosphere. Plus, keeping things turned off helps reduce your family's electric bill.

BE A HERO!

If you've stopped using something, don't just turn it off—unplug it, too. When an appliance is plugged in, it is still using some electricity regardless of whether it's turned on or off.

4 TURN OFF THE TAP

Whether you're brushing your teeth, lathering soap on your hands, shampooing your hair, or washing the dishes, turning the tap off while you do it will conserve water—and energy, if you're running the hot tap.

DON'T WASH THE DISHES AS OFTEN!

You'll love this one! Rinse dishes quickly and leave them to one side until there are enough to make running a full sink of hot water worthwhile. Using a dishwasher, if you have one, is even better— they use less water than washing by hand. But only put the dishwasher on when it's full, as it uses the same amount of water and electricity regardless of load size.

HOW MUCH?

The average person living in a developed country uses about 2,000 gallons (9,000 liters) of water a day. That's about as much as a cement mixer truck holds! Most of this water (95 percent) is used to produce the food we eat.

5 SHUT THAT DOOR!

It might feel like you're just being nagged, but there's a very good reason your grown-ups say this! Warm air escapes through open doors and windows, so not only are you wasting heat energy, you are also wasting money. Closing blinds and curtains helps keep the warmth in during the winter months, too— and keeping them shut in the summer can help keep your home cool, reducing the need for electric fans or air-conditioning units.

6 MAKE THE MOST OF PAPER

Though paper is recyclable, renewable, and pretty cheap, the processes behind making it—and recycling it—use a lot of energy and natural resources. Plus, paper can only be recycled around six times before the fibers become too damaged to bond properly. Get lots of use out of the paper you have by using both sides before recycling!

When we print less we:

- ✓ Save trees
- ✓ Waste less energy
- ✓ Cut carbon emissions
- ✓ Reduce water pollution
- ✓ Create less waste!

STAY SUPER!

Reducing the amount of paper you use keeps our trees doing what they do best—providing lovely fresh oxygen for us to breathe and absorbing carbon dioxide from our atmosphere, which helps keep our planet cool.

7 MAKE A "NO JUNK MAIL" SIGN

Junk mail has a massive carbon footprint. More than 100 million trees are destroyed each year to make junk mail—and then most of it just goes in the trash!

Make an eye-catching sign to put near your mailbox to let people know you don't want any junk mail. Your parents can also fill in forms online. These steps should help reduce the amount you receive. You might still get some, so be sure to recycle what you can.

8 CREATE A HOMEMADE SCRAPBOOK

One way to reduce the amount of paper you throw away is to use it to make something else instead. This cute little scrapbook is created from sheets of paper otherwise destined for the recycling bin.

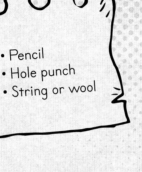

You will need:
- Scraps of paper
- Used cereal box
- Scissors
- Ruler
- Pencil
- Hole punch
- String or wool

❶ Trim the scraps of paper into squares approximately 4 in. x 4 in. (10 cm x 10 cm)—or whatever size you want your book to be—then cut two pieces of cardboard from the cereal box to make the cover. Assemble the front and back covers with the paper in the middle to create an unbound book.

You might need to punch in sections if you have lots of sheets of paper.

❷ Use your ruler to draw a line down the left edge of the front cover, about 1/2 in. (1 cm) in. Make a mark every 1 in. (2.5 cm) or so along this line, and use the hole punch to create holes where the marks are.

❸ Thread the string through the holes in whatever pattern you want and tie securely with a knot. Done! What will you use your hand-recycled scrapbook for?

You can use your book as either a notebook or scrapbook, depending on how plain the paper is.

9 TURN OFF YOUR SCREENS!

You might think that a little screen time won't harm the environment. However, the servers that run search engines and apps generate a massive amount of CO_2—and, of course, keeping your device charged up uses energy. So turn off and help the planet by having some good old-fashioned fun!

Here are some suggestions for a fun day of digital detoxing:

Make up a dance

Play cards or a board game

Learn a new skill, maybe a language or how to knit

Plan a family meal and help make it

Tidy your room

Play hopscotch

Read a book

Do a jigsaw

Bake some bread, cookies, or a cake

Create a puppet show

Traditional electric power plants create electricity by burning fossil fuels.

HOW IS ELECTRICITY MADE?

Electricity is often created by burning fossil fuels such as oil, coal, and natural gas. They are called fossil fuels because they are the remains of plants and animals that lived—and died—a very long time ago. The problem with burning fossil fuels, other than the pollution it causes, is that they are not sustainable, meaning one day they will run out. So we need to explore ways of making electricity from things that won't run out instead, such as solar energy and wind power.

Wind turbines generate electricity as the blades rotate.

Large panels on a solar farm convert the sun's energy into electricity.

A random act of kindness is something you do for someone else simply to make them happy. Making someone else happy makes you feel good, too!

Paint family portraits

Do a random act of kindness

Set up a treasure hunt

RECYCLING AND UPCYCLING

Most people recycle some of their trash, but too much still ends up in a landfill. Around 80 percent of all waste could actually be recycled, but we only recycle around half of it. So how can you and those around you help to get this figure higher?

10 RECYCLING VS. LANDFILL

Most things that get thrown away go to a landfill. A landfill site is a big hole in the ground where trash is piled. When the pile gets too big, the site is closed and usually covered over with soil, and further trash will get sent to a new one.

Some of the trash in a landfill site decomposes over time, releasing harmful gases into the air and chemicals into the ground. But other trash doesn't decompose at all, and will stay there forever.

A landfill site in Thailand

Not all trash goes to a landfill. Instead, some of it gets burned in large incinerating ovens, and the heat energy is converted into electricity. This might sound like a good plan, but burning some materials (such as plastic) pumps nasty chemicals into the air.

Widely recycled :-)

- Paper/cardboard— magazines, newspapers, leaflets, junk mail, cardboard boxes, food boxes, empty bath tissue rolls, plain greeting cards
- Plastic—bottles, jugs, tubs, trays
- Metal—food and beverage cans, aerosol cans, aluminum foil, caps, lids
- Glass — bottles, jars

RECYCLE WHAT YOU CAN

The good news is that most of our waste can be recycled. Exactly which items can be recycled through your local collection varies from area to area, but, generally speaking, paper, glass, plastic, and aluminum can be recycled everywhere. Other items may also be recyclable where you live —ask your parents if you can look at your local council's website to check.

Check locally :-|

- Plastic bags
- Ink cartridges
- Coffee pods
- Plastic wrap
- Food waste
- Potato chip bags
- Batteries

Can't be recycled :-(

- Polystyrene trays
- Sticky tape
- Foil wrapping paper
- Glitter
- Wet wipes
- Tissues
- Foil pouches
- Diapers
- Plastic cutlery
- Plastic straws

11 IF IT'S BROKEN, FIX IT!

If your favorite toy, a household tool, or an item of clothing is broken or not working anymore—don't fear! Check whether it can be fixed before throwing it away. Do some research online, or ask an adult for ideas. If you're still stumped, consider checking whether there are any repair cafés or community "fix it" events in your area. These are run by volunteers who will show you what the problem is and help you repair it.

SET UP AN EVENT

If you can't find a repair café or event in your area, speak to your school or grown-ups about organizing one.

BE A HERO!

Mending things instead of throwing them away or recycling them is much better for the environment—fewer materials and less energy are used when you fix up what you already have. It saves you (or your family) money, too!

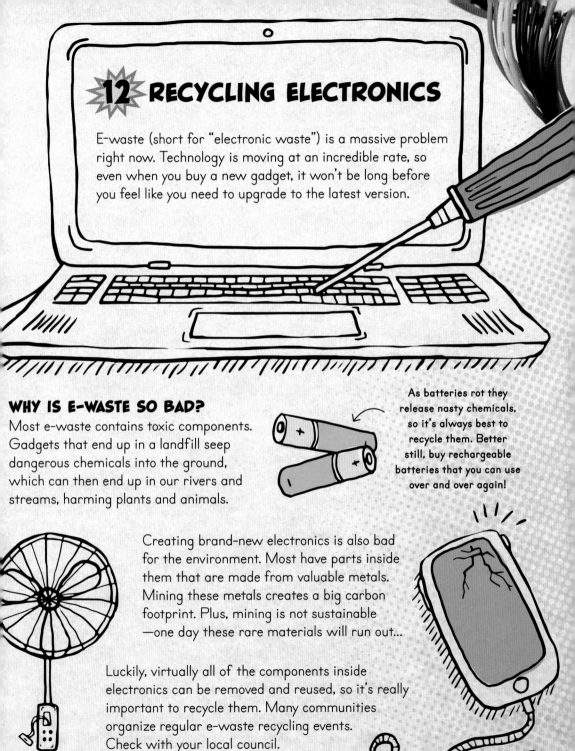

12 RECYCLING ELECTRONICS

E-waste (short for "electronic waste") is a massive problem right now. Technology is moving at an incredible rate, so even when you buy a new gadget, it won't be long before you feel like you need to upgrade to the latest version.

WHY IS E-WASTE SO BAD?

Most e-waste contains toxic components. Gadgets that end up in a landfill seep dangerous chemicals into the ground, which can then end up in our rivers and streams, harming plants and animals.

As batteries rot they release nasty chemicals, so it's always best to recycle them. Better still, buy rechargeable batteries that you can use over and over again!

Creating brand-new electronics is also bad for the environment. Most have parts inside them that are made from valuable metals. Mining these metals creates a big carbon footprint. Plus, mining is not sustainable —one day these rare materials will run out...

Luckily, virtually all of the components inside electronics can be removed and reused, so it's really important to recycle them. Many communities organize regular e-waste recycling events. Check with your local council.

13 FROM TRASH TO TREASURE

Wait a minute! Do you HAVE to put that old cereal box and empty baked bean can in the recycling? Before you throw things away, think about whether you can make them into something else. Here are some really simple ideas to get you started—a quick online search will help you discover tons more...

SAFETY FIRST!

Before you start, make sure your cans have no sharp edges. And always ask for adult help when using sharp tools.

TIN CAN TREASURE

Funky Pencil Pot

Remove paper labels and wrap a strip of colorful fabric around a can, using PVA to glue it in place. When it's dry, paint another layer of PVA over the top to strengthen it.

The fabric strip can be cut out of old clothes that would otherwise get thrown away.

Be sure to only place the lantern on a heat-safe surface, and of course only light the candle with adult supervision.

Outdoor Lantern

For this craft you'll definitely need the help of a grown-up.

Fill an empty tin can with water and stand it upright in the freezer overnight. Once frozen, lay the can on a folded towel to stop it sliding around. Using a hammer and sharp nails, gently punch holes through the can to make a pattern. Then melt the ice and put a mini-candle inside.

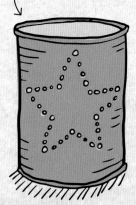

CARDBOARD CREATIONS

Cereal Box Gift Bag

Standing an empty, open cereal box upright, pinch the smaller sides inward to create a vertical crease down the center of each side. Then carefully cut the top off the box and discard. Cover the box with pages from an old magazine or wrapping paper, punch two holes in the front and back, and thread through some ribbon or string to make a handle.

Card Bookmarks

Cut old, colorful greetings cards into strips, punch a hole at one end, and tie through some ribbon or string. You'll never lose your place again!

You can also make gift tags in this way!

GLASS GIFTS

Jam Jar Vase

Remove the labels from an empty jam jar and paint a band of PVA glue around the middle. Wrap string, colored wool, thread, or ribbon around the glued area until it's covered, then wait for it to dry. Fill the jar with water and add some flowers. Voilà!

Sweet Treats

Fill a clean jar with colorful candy, homemade caramel corn, or chocolates and put the lid back on. Use permanent markers, scraps of old material, or patterned paper to personalize the jar and lid, and create a lovely present for a friend.

PLASTIC'S NOT FANTASTIC

Plastic is one of our planet's biggest problems right now. But fear not, with the help of our eco-heroes we can sort this out!

14 AVOID SINGLE-USE PLASTIC

Single-use plastic is exactly that—plastic that gets used once, then thrown away. Water bottles, plastic wrappers, and plastic shopping bags are all guilty culprits. We might not think too much about buying a bottle of our favorite drink when we're out, or asking for a plastic bag at the checkout, but these choices seriously impact our planet.

Almost all plastics are made from chemicals that come from fossil fuels such as oil, gas, and coal. Then, once it's been used, not all plastic can be recycled, so it ends up in a landfill or gets incinerated, both of which release dangerous gases.

STAY SUPER!

You can help reduce plastic waste by not buying items that come with free plastic toys and food that comes in plastic packaging.

These single-use plastic items...

Straws
Cutlery
Plastic cups
Disposable beverage bottles
Plastic wrap

Could be replaced with these...

Paper or reusable straws
Wooden cutlery or household knives and forks
Paper cups or household cups
Refillable water bottles
Beeswax wraps or reusable containers

SAVE OUR SEA LIFE!

Our oceans are riddled with plastic. Every year more than eight million tons of plastic ends up in the sea—that works out to be about a truck-full every minute! It's believed there are now more than five trillion plastic items throughout the world's oceans, and unless things change, by 2050 there will be more plastic than fish. That's a scary thought.

The Great Pacific Garbage Patch is a mass of floating garbage that has built up in the ocean between Japan and North America. It is almost double the size of Texas!

BE A HERO!

The next time you visit a beach, keep an eye out for any plastic waste. If it's safe to do so, pick it up and take it to be recycled. See pages 70–71 for more litter-picking tips.

Because plastic is lightweight, it gets blown around and ends up in streams, rivers, and on the beach. This is how so much of it ends up in our seas. And it doesn't decompose like paper or food —instead, it just keeps breaking into tinier and tinier pieces, until it becomes microplastic. "Microplastic" is a term given to pieces of plastic smaller than 0.2 in. (5 mm). Fish and other sea animals can't tell the difference between microplastic and small bits of food, so they eat it.

15 GIVE UP THE GUM!

Thousands of tons of plastic waste actually comes from our mouths in the form of chewing gum. Gum is actually made of the stuff—yuck! Once the flavor's gone, it just ends up in the trash—or worse still—on the ground, where it can be picked up and eaten by animals.

To conquer the problem of gum pollution, some manufacturers are now making gum from natural ingredients. And some places have specific gum bins to recycle it into other items like reusable cups, combs, and rain boots!

16 HOST A PLASTIC-FREE PARTY!

Who doesn't love a party? Getting together with your friends and family to celebrate a birthday or other special occasion is a lot of fun, but parties can be heavy on plastic waste and not very kind to the planet. Hosting your own plastic-free party means you might also inspire others to do the same!

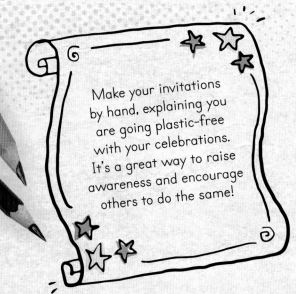

Make your invitations by hand, explaining you are going plastic-free with your celebrations. It's a great way to raise awareness and encourage others to do the same!

Replace plastic toys in goodie bags with more ecological items. Colored pencils, wildflower seeds, or a small book, plus a cute origami animal you've made yourself, are all nice choices.

Instead of balloons and banners, make some homemade decorations. Paper chains, pom-poms, and flags made from scrap fabric are all great ways to brighten up your party space. They can all be reused, too!

FOOD WASTE

GENERAL WASTE

RECYCLING ONLY

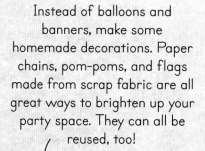

Make sure your bins are clearly labeled so your guests know where to put any waste.

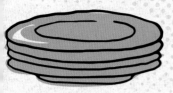

Consider using household dishes and cutlery. If you're a bit worried about breakages, then paper plates are a much better choice than plastic ones.

Provide food that isn't individually wrapped. Plan how much you'll need per person—and stick to it!

17 GIVE NON-PLASTIC PRESENTS

If someone else is doing the celebrating, go eco with your choice of present and card. Homemade treats, books, fabric or wooden toys, clothes (from natural materials), or vouchers/tickets are all environmentally friendly ideas and can be adjusted to suit any budget.

AND CARDS

A handmade, personalized card means much more to the person receiving it than a store-bought one. It's also less likely to be thrown in the trash when the celebrating is over. Just avoid using glitter!

BE A HERO!

Metallic wrapping paper contains plastic, so create your own instead. Use a roll of brown paper and print a pattern on it using leaves or stamps you have made from cut potatoes or household items, or simply decorate the paper with pens and pencils. And instead of using sticky tape, use eco-friendly paper or washi tape and string, wool, or ribbon to wrap the present up.

10 today!

YOU'RE A

PLASTIC BOTTLE CRAFTS

These easy crafts are a fun way to reuse plastic bottles and turn them into something useful!

Bowling Game

This is a really simple craft, which is both fun to make and play with afterwards. Your biggest challenge is likely to be sourcing the disposable bottles, as eco-heroes rarely buy them!

You will need:
- Ten plastic bottles, all the same size and style
- Paper or fabric to decorate
- A fairly weighted ball

Stick a piece of paper or fabric around the middle of each bottle, then number them with a thick marker. Pour in around 2 in. (5 cm) of water to make sure they don't fall over too easily, then put the lids back on. Challenge your friends — the winner could either be the player who knocks down the most, or the person who gets the highest score by adding up the numbers.

You can ask your friends, family, and school to save any bottles they use.

Indoor Herb Garden

Fresh herbs smell gorgeous and taste delicious! Grow some of your own in planters on a bright windowsill.

You will need:
- Large plastic beverage bottles (3.5 pints / 2 liters)
- Old newspaper or magazine
- PVA glue, a brush, and scissors
- Soil and a selection of growing herbs

Carefully cut around the middle of each of your plastic bottles, about 1 (2 or 3 cm) above halfway. Turn the tops of the bottles over, place them inside the bottoms, and use strong tape to hold them in place. Tear strip from a newspaper or magazine and use the PVA to completely cover the outside of the planters with the strips. Once dry, fill your pots with soil and herb plants—basil, mint, and chives all grow well in a sunny spot.

Bird Feeder

Make your garden more attractive to birds by providing them with a tasty snack. Ask for a grown-up's help with this craft, as cutting the holes in the bottle can be tricky.

Cut a small circle roughly the same diameter as your stick 1.5 in. (3 cm) from the bottom of the bottle. Repeat on the other side and push your stick through both holes. Create two more small holes 1.5 in. (3 cm) above the stick—these will be the holes the birds feed from. Using the pin, carefully pierce the base of the bottle to create drain holes. Fill the bottle with seed, put the lid on, and tie some string around the neck.

Hang your bottle from a tree, in a sheltered location, and use books or the internet to help you identify the birds that visit!

You will need:
- A clean, dry plastic bottle
- A stick, about 4 in. (10 cm) longer than the bottle is wide
- Scissors or craft knife
- Pin
- String
- Bird seed

Putting the top of the bottle inside the bottom means excess water will drain through the neck and create a reservoir of water for when the plant needs it.

REDUCE, REUSE, RECYCLE

You may have heard the motto **"Reduce, Reuse, Recycle."** But what does it mean exactly?

1. **Reduce** what we buy and use. This is the best way to tackle plastic waste.

2. **Reuse** is exactly what you are doing by making these crafts; reusing the waste by turning it into something else.

3. **Recycle.** When you can't do the above, recycle.

CLOTHES

Fashion is one of the most wasteful industries in the world. We are constantly encouraged to "keep up with the trends" and buy new items, but it's really not good for our planet. Read on to find plenty of ways to get creative with your clothes instead!

19 REVAMP OLD CLOTHES

We all have favorite—and not-so-favorite—items of clothing. Rather than throw away the pieces you don't love anymore, transform them and give them a new lease on life.

Changing buttons, gluing on patches, or altering the length of something (ask a grown-up to help with this) are all easy ways to update your clothes. You can find loads more hacks online, and many of them don't require any sewing skills, like iron-on patches. You'll end up with a whole wardrobe full of individual, one-of-a-kind pieces while feeling good about saving the planet.

A truckload of clothing ends up in a landfill **every second!**

Three-fifths of all clothes get thrown away within a year of being bought!

Only I percent of material is recycled into something else!

COLOR CHANGING

Go for a festival vibe by tie-dying some old, plain white clothes. You can buy kits containing everything you need, or you can use rubber bands and natural dyes for a really eco-version.

Natural materials, such as cotton and linen, work best.

Check out how many different colored dyes you can make naturally—you'll be amazed!

Orange – carrots

Pink – red rose petals, avocado skins and seeds (sounds weird, but it's true!)

Gray – blackberries

Yellow – turmeric, dandelion flowers

Brown – tea or coffee

Blue – red cabbage (seriously!)

20 CREATE A COSTUME

Whether it's a school play, your best friend's fancy dress birthday party, or Halloween, homemade costumes are WAY more original than store-bought ones—and if you're using up old clothes, they are kinder to the planet. Grab a pair of scissors and a few safety pins and let your imagination run wild!

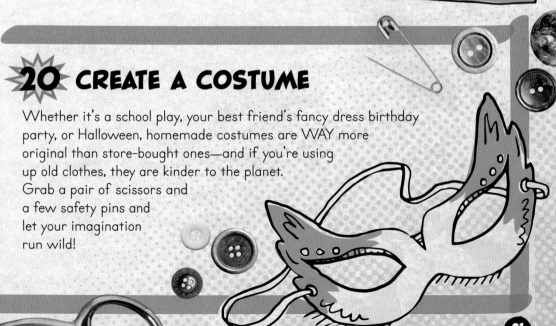

21 MAKE A T-SHIRT TOTE BAG

You will need:
• An old T-shir
• Fabric scissor
• Felt tip pen
• Ruler

Create a reusable tote bag from an old T-shirt. No sewing required, just a pair of sharp fabric scissors—and the ability to tie lots of knots!

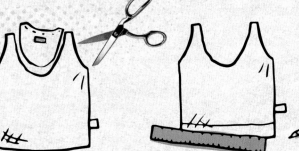

1 Turn the T-shirt inside out and cut the sleeves off.

2 Cut a semi-circle to remove the neck area, creating a nice big opening to your bag.

3 With a ruler, draw a horizontal line across the T-shirt, about 3 in. (8 cm) from the bottom.

4 Cut slits through both layers of fabric, from the bottom of the T-shirt up to the line, about 1 in. (2 or 3 cm) apart, to create a fringe of strips across the bottom. Starting from the left, tie each pair of strips together in double knots.

5 Once all pairs are tied, return to the left and tie each pair of strips to the pair next to it. This will block the holes that were left between each pair in the previous stage.

6 Turn your T-shirt right side out again and you have yourself a *tote-ally* funky new bag!

If you've not got an old T-shirt yourself, ask around or pick one up from a thrift store.

22 DONATE

If you can't reuse your clothes yourself, pass them on. You might have a younger sibling, cousin, or friend who would like them. Or you could give them to a thrift store, clothing bank, or local children's group. There are lots of organizations that will take donations and pass them on to families who need them, or sell them in shops to raise funds. Just make sure they are clean first.

You could also find out whether there are any children's clothing libraries in your area. These work in the same way as book libraries; clothes are borrowed and then returned when they have been outgrown, saving parents money and saving the planet, too.

STAY SUPER!

Old clothes can be reused in so many different ways, and not just to make something new to wear. The Internet is full of creative ideas—sites like Pinterest are a great place to start.

CREATE A HAVEN FOR WILDLIFE

Be a friend to nature by creating the perfect spot for bees, birds, and bugs.

23 PLANT PLANTS FOR POLLINATORS

Did you know that nearly all the fruit and vegetables we eat need pollinators to grow? A pollinator carries pollen from plant to plant, helping them reproduce. Bees are fantastic pollinators because they collect nectar and pollen to make honey.

Ask an adult to help you find out which nectar-rich flowers are native to your area. Plant a selection in your garden or in a window box for bees and other insects to enjoy.

Once you've created your bee-friendly patch, remember to look after it by watering it regularly. You can also keep your flowers extra happy by feeding them your very own natural plant food (see page 41)!

24 HELP A BEE IN NEED

If you spot a bumblebee on the ground, it's probably just resting. Buzzing about all day collecting nectar and pollen can be quite exhausting! If you think it might get trodden on, use a leaf to move it to a safer place.

However, if the bee is still there after 45 minutes, it might be too tired to fly. Become a bug rescuer and carefully move it to a bee-friendly flower to feed. If there are none around, create a sugar-water mix (half white sugar, half water) and place a spoonful next to the bee. This might just be the boost it needs to recover and fly away!

SAVE THE BEES

Bees are vital to our food chain, but their numbers are declining. Their natural habitats are being destroyed, and more pesticides are being used on crops. By helping the bees we are also helping ourselves—we can't grow fruit and vegetables without them!

BE A HERO!

If honey is your thing, be sure to buy local. Keep carbon emissions down and support local beekeepers by avoiding mass-produced honey which might have been made using aggressive farming methods.

HONEY

25 CREATE A MINI-POND

Bees and flying insects might like a bright and airy flower patch, but there are many other creatures that prefer something a bit damper. Convert a corner of your garden into a mini-pond or wet area by burying a large container, such as an old sink or baby bathtub, in the ground. Fill it with water (rainwater is best as it doesn't contain chemicals), then add some clean gravel, rocks, and water plants. Layer more stones around the outside to create a few damp, shady spots for the wildlife to take cover.

SAFETY FIRST!

Even mini-ponds can be dangerous to small children, so make sure your pond is positioned somewhere safe, where no one can trip and fall in.

Creatures your pond might attract:

Water snails

Frogs

Dragonflies

Butterflies

Birds

Water beetles

Water striders

If you don't have much outdoor space, you can create a very small pond in a large plant pot or an old shallow bowl (but not your family's best serving dish!).

BE A HERO!

Make sure wildlife can get in and out easily by using rocks or logs to create a path for them.

26 MAKE A BUG HOTEL

No matter what size your garden is—or even if you don't have one—you can still create a wonderful space for creatures to explore. A bug hotel can be made from all kinds of garden and household waste; just add a few natural materials, and you'll have a shelter full of hidey-holes for all kinds of wildlife.

You will need:
- Wood pallets or a plant pot
- A selection of the following items: bricks, stones, broken roof tiles, dead wood, bark, logs, old plant pots, twigs, moss, dry leaves, straw, pine cones, plastic bottles, hollow plant stems, old pipes, corrugated cardboard

1 Choose a partly shady, partly sunny spot, with firm, level ground.

2 Lay the pallets on top of each other, making sure they are secure and don't wobble. Tie them together with some string if you need to.

3 Fill the gaps with whatever you want! There are no rules, but certain materials attract certain creatures...

Dead wood attracts wood-boring beetles, spiders, and woodlice.

If you don't have much space, use an old plant pot on its side instead.

Ladybugs love to hibernate under dry leaves.

Corrugated cardboard rolled up inside plastic bottles provides a great home for lacewings.

STAY SUPER!

You can build a bug hotel at any time of year, but you might find the materials are easier to lay your hands on in fall. This is also when lots of creatures are looking for the perfect spot to hibernate over winter.

Hollow stems, pipes, and bricks with holes are great places for solitary bees to lay their eggs.

GET GREEN-FINGERED

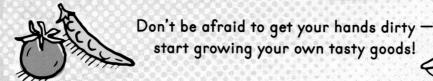

Don't be afraid to get your hands dirty —
start growing your own tasty goods!

27 GROW YOUR OWN

By growing your own fruit and vegetables you are "going green" in more ways than one. Homegrown food is packaging-free, transportation-free, and pesticide-free, plus, it tastes AMAZING!

Luckily, you can grow fruit and vegetables anywhere! If you don't have much room, grow container crops like lettuce or strawberries. Sunshine-loving plants such as tomatoes and peppers grow well in a bright, sunny spot. And if you have a raised bed, grow veggies that need deep soil like carrots and potatoes.

START SIMPLE
If you've never grown your own fruit and vegetables before, begin with easy-to-grow crops like tomatoes, green beans, and zucchini.

You can grow your crops from seed, or buy young plants from a garden center in the spring. Young plants will need to be kept indoors at first, but you can then gradually get them used to being outdoors before finally planting them where you'd like them to grow. Some crops, like beets and radishes, don't like being moved, so it's best to sow these seeds where you plan to grow them.

GO BIG!

If you enjoy growing your own food but need a bit more space, ask your family to find out whether there are community gardens near your home. You need to be prepared to visit often—your fruit and vegetables will need to be regularly watered and looked after—but you'll pick up lots of tips from other growers and be able to swap plants and crops as well!

You will need:
- Large pots, grow bags, a raised bed, or a patch of soil
- Seeds or young plants
- Compost (see page 40)
- Hand fork
- Trowel
- Watering can

SHARE THE LOVE
If you have a bumper crop, give some to a friend or neighbor. You'll be helping the planet even more as they won't need to go to the supermarket to buy their own!

28 COMPOSTING

Compost is a type of fertilizer made from rotting plants and household waste, so it's very easy and cheap to produce. All you need is a composting bin—you can use any old big container for this—or you could ask a grown-up to help you make one from old wood pallets or chicken wire.

Keep topping the bin up, and your compost will be ready to use after a few months.

Composting bins work best when the items are layered.

Put these items in your composting bin:

- Fruit and vegetable scraps
- Moldy fruit and vegetables
- Coffee grounds
- Tea bags
- Straw
- Sawdust from untreated wood
- Paper towels and tissues
- Grass cuttings
- Fallen leaves
- Shredded paper
- Eggshells

But don't be tempted to include any of these:

- Meat scraps and processed food (they attract rats)
- Diseased plants (the compost might spread the disease to the new plants you grow)
- Pet poop (just yuck!)

29 MAKE PLANT FOOD

Plants need water, sunshine, and food to grow and survive. But store-bought plant food can contain chemicals that harm insects and contaminate water sources. Make your own eco-fertilizer from food waste.

Stir coffee grounds with water and pour it on your plants, or mix the grounds directly into the soil. This makes the earth more acidic, which plants such as tomatoes, roses, and blueberries love.

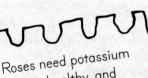

Roses need potassium to stay healthy, and bananas are full of it! Bury banana peel around the base of a rosebush to help protect it from frost and diseases.

Dig washed, crushed eggshells into the soil. Eggshells are full of calcium, which helps plants grow strong. Some people think it also helps keep slugs and snails away from your plants.

You could also make a plant food superhero smoothie, mixing coffee grounds, banana peel, and eggshells together in a blender with some water. Your fruit and vegetable plants will never have felt so good!

30 RECYCLE RAINWATER

A good way to save water is to, well, save water! By collecting rainwater in a rain barrel or even a large bucket, you won't need to turn on the tap to give the plants a drink. Plus, rainwater contains fewer chemicals than tap water, so your plants should thrive on it!

OUT AND ABOUT

Stepping out into your neighborhood to make changes can be daunting: where do you start? First, put on your eco-hero goggles! With a new sense of awareness, you'll start to see how you can interact with the world around you kindly and responsibly.

EXPLORE YOUR AREA

Saving the planet doesn't need to be boring. After all, superheroes lead pretty exciting lives, and eco-heroes are no different. Get outside and enjoy this wonderful world we call home!

31 TAKE A PUBLIC TRANSIT ROAD TRIP

Organize a road trip with a difference. Take a train, bus, streetcar, or ferry—or even a combination of all four—and explore further afield while leaving the car at home. With a grown-up's help, use the Internet to do your research: choose a destination, plan your route, and check timetables online before you set off.

TRAVEL GAMES

Using public transit sometimes means there's a bit of hanging around, so have a couple of game ideas up your sleeve. If I-Spy leaves you rolling your eyes and muttering "not again," try one of these other activities to pass the time instead...

Twenty Questions

An old classic! One player thinks of something and everyone takes turns to ask questions to figure out what it is. Up to 20 questions can be asked in total, and they can only be answered with a yes or no.

The Alphabet Game

Using place names you see on road signs, work your way through the alphabet. A is for Albany, B is for Boston, C is for Chicago and so on...

Albany

Boston

Is there somewhere local you've never ventured to, a few footpaths you haven't walked down, a café nearby that you've heard has THE BEST caramel cookie milkshakes? Exploring your local area means fewer carbon emissions are pumped into the atmosphere, as you and your family won't be driving as far—if at all. Plus, you'll be doing your bit to support your local community.

The Word Association Game

The first player says a word—any word—then the second player says a word associated with it. Then the next player says a word associated with the last word, and so on. If a player hesitates or repeats a word, they're out.

For example: grass, green, frog, hop, skip, rope, ladder...

Ribbit!

Spot It!

You need a pen or pencil and some paper for this one. Make a list for each player of items to spot on the journey, and the first one to find them all is the winner.

The License Plate Game

Make up sentences using the letters from license plates. MM21 LCS could be Molly Mara Loves Chocolate Spread or My Mom Likes Crazy Sunglasses!

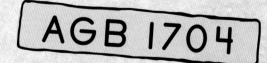

Ahmed's Gone Bananas!

33 DITCH THE CAR!

Whenever you go to a store, park, or school, or spend some time with your friends, try to stop yourself from asking your folks to drive you there. Get your bike or scooter out and take to your wheels—or simply walk. If the weather is wet, don't let it dampen your spirits. Just put on a coat and some waterproof boots and enjoy splashing in puddles!

SUPER SENSES!

Make a walk more interesting by really absorbing what's going on around you. It's amazing what details you'll notice when you make a conscious effort to be more aware...

Walk slowly and look closely. Can you see a spider busily weaving a web, beautiful architecture above a storefront, or animal tracks in the mud?

Listen carefully. Are you able to hear birds singing, a babbling stream, or a baby crying?

Breathe deeply. What can you smell? Flowers, wet asphalt—or maybe your local takeout preparing a tasty treat?

Think about the ground beneath your feet. How does it feel? Is it squishy, crunchy, or hard?

34 GO ON A BIKE RIDE

Cycling is a great activity to do as a family or with friends, and it causes virtually no environmental damage, making it a number-one activity for eco-heroes. Plan a route that avoids busy roads and, if it's a long trip, take plenty of water and snacks and plan in advance where you might stop for a break.

STAY SUPER!

Ask a grown-up to make sure your bike is in tip-top condition before you set out. That means inflating the tires, testing the brakes, and maybe putting a bit of oil on the chain—especially if its been a while since you last used it!

If you don't own a bike already, fear not—there are plenty of places you can rent one. Many cities now have convenient schemes that allow you to pick up a bike from one location and leave it at another. If you get the cycling bug, you could consider buying a reconditioned used bike—it's cheaper than buying a new one!

City cycles can be rented via an app on a smart phone.

SAFETY FIRST!

Always wear a helmet when cycling and make sure you have working front and rear lights. A bell is also handy if you're cycling near pedestrians.

35 GO KAYAKING, CANOEING, OR PADDLE-BOARDING

Kayaking, canoeing, and paddle-boarding are fantastic forms of planet-friendly fun. Unlike motorboats, they require no gas or oil, and the slower speeds are much kinder to wildlife and the surrounding environment. They are also great forms of exercise.

All you need to get started is a river, lake, or seafront area with a watersports center where you can rent the equipment, including life jackets. Not many people have their own equipment to begin with, so renting everything you need is a cheap way to see if you like it.

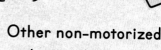

SAFETY FIRST!

Open water is dangerous. Always make sure you have a responsible adult with you!

Help protect the environment:

- Carry your kayak, canoe, or paddle-board in or out of the water instead of dragging it, so you don't damage the environment.
- While on land, stick to pathways and designated launch areas.
- Try to avoid using the paddles in very shallow water as these areas can contain fish spawn.
- The quieter you are, the fewer creatures you'll disturb—meaning you'll get a much better view of the wildlife!
- Keep away from animals nesting on riverbanks.
- Report any pollution you spot.

Other non-motorized watersports to try:

Rowing

Sailing

Pedaloes

Tubing

Rafting

Open water swimming

If you do get a taste for any of th
paddle sports, think about getting
membership with an organizatior
that encourages paddling respons
and helps fund improvements to
local environment.

36 GO SURFING OR BODYBOARDING

If you're lucky enough to live or go on vacation near the coast, nothing beats spending time in, or on, the sea. But instead of heading out on an engine-powered boat trip, why don't you learn how to surf, bodyboard, or windsurf instead? Many surfing hot spots offer lessons, and you can rent all the equipment from the organizations running them, too.

ECO-EQUIPMENT

Cheap surfboards and bodyboards are made with nasty chemicals and polystyrene balls that pollute the sea if they break. So instead of buying a cheap board, rent a board instead. Rented boards tend to be of a higher quality and are less likely to break—better still, check whether they are made from organic materials like wood, bamboo, or cork.

BE SUN SAFE!

It's really important to protect your skin from the sun. Using an eco-friendly sunscreen is a great way to stay safe while also preventing nasty chemicals from getting into the sea (and your skin!).

Wetsuits and surf wax are typically made from non-eco materials, but companies are starting to offer more planet-friendly options, so try and use these when you can.

ECO WAX

BE A HERO!

Leave the beach as nature intended. Pebbles, sand, and shells should stay there, but of course feel free to take home any litter you spot! Find litter-picking tips on pages 70–71.

37 HAVE A LITTER-FREE PICNIC

There's nothing better than a picnic on a summer's day. But alfresco dining can also create a lot of waste—squeezy juice cartons and single-use cutlery will just end up in a landfill.

Invest in some beeswax wraps for your fruit and vegetables. These work like plastic wrap, but can be washed and reused.

Pack sandwiches and pasta salads in washable plastic containers.

Swap disposable plastic drinks for reusable water bottles.

STAY SUPER!

While it's better to use washable containers, glass is best left at home. Accidents do happen, and broken glass can be really harmful to wildlife—and humans!

WAIT TO WASH

If you're having the kind of picnic that involves plates and cutlery, make sure it's all washable; bring along reusable plastic plates and metal cutlery, then wrap it all up and take it home to wash when you're finished.

Instead of buying lots of small bags of potato chips, crackers, or popcorn, buy one large bag and share it.

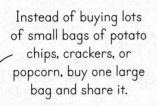

CHEESY SNACKS

BE A HERO!

Instead of taking wet wipes to your picnic, pack a dishcloth from home and wet it with a splash of water to wipe your sticky fingers.

WIPE OUT WET WIPES!

So, what's the problem with wet wipes? Most wipes are made from a type of plastic that can't be recycled. Wipes can't be flushed down the toilet either because they don't break down, meaning they can cause blockages or end up in the sea. The only option left is to put them in the trash. Many marine conservation organizations are trying to completely ban the sale of wet wipes containing plastic and make sure that non-plastic wipes are safe to flush.

CLEAN UP!

Once the fun is over, remember to take any trash you have created home with you. Even if there are trash cans at the picnic site, they can get full and overflow quickly.

38 EAT OUT RESPONSIBLY

Grabbing a snack or meal while you're out and about shouldn't cost the Earth. Make these small changes every time you eat out, and feel good that you are doing your bit to help save the planet.

PLASTIC STRAWS SUCK!

Plastic straws can't be recycled and they don't biodegrade (break down naturally)—and they aren't even necessary. The good news is that some countries have already banned the sale of plastic straws, and if we all refuse to use them, one day they will be no more than a distant memory...

TAKE YOUR OWN CUP

Disposable cups, especially those lined in plastic, are a big problem. Thankfully, mo and more coffee shops are recognizing th and are happy to fill a customer's own cu if they bring one along.

CUTLERY-FREE TAKEOUT

You might never have thought that the humble sandwich could be the perfect eco-friendly takeout lunch! If it's created while you wait, it requires no plastic packaging, plus, you don't need disposable cutlery to eat it. Perfect!

SAY NO TO SACHETS

Cute little packets of ketchup or mayo might be convenient, but they have a huge environmental impact. Polluting chemicals are used to make them and, because sachets are not recyclable, they have to go in the trash. This means the chemicals end up in the ground if the sachets go to a landfill or in the air if they are burned—or they get carried on the wind and end up in the sea, harming ocean life.

So while it's easy to grab and go, if bottles of ketchup or mayo are available, consider using them instead. Then give yourself a pat on the back for doing your bit!

IF YOU'RE NOT IMPRESSED, ASK FOR CHANGE

If you think the place you're eating at could do better at eliminating unnecessary waste, let the owner or manager know! Ask a grown-up to help you write an e-mail, politely telling them why plastic waste is bad and suggesting the changes they could make. Sometimes people just need a reminder that they could do better!

USE RECYCLING BINS

Most restaurants, cafés, and takeouts have recycling bins, so sort your waste before you head off. Just be sure to put the right items in the right bins!

GO SHOPPING, ECO-STYLE!

How to shop and save the Earth at the same time!

39 GO TO A FARMERS' MARKET

With so many tasty foods on offer, a farmers' market is a feast for the senses! It's also a more planet-friendly way of shopping compared to buying groceries from a large supermarket.

HERE'S WHY...

• Many farmers who sell their produce at markets use organic farming methods, which means they use fewer chemicals to grow their crops.

• Fruit and vegetables are usually sold loose, which means there's no packaging to throw away. Also, because it's all sold loose, you can just buy what you need, meaning there's less food waste.

• Food is grown locally. It hasn't had to rely on being transported halfway around the world, so it has a much smaller carbon footprint than the fruit and vegetables imported and sold at a supermarket.

• Local fruit and vegetables are often fresher and tastier. Food that has traveled hundreds of miles will have been picked earlier than food from only a few miles away.

• Buying direct from the farmer means you are supporting your local community rather than multimillion-dollar businesses.

NOT JUST FRUIT AND VEGETABLES
Farmers' markets often sell other items, too, such as locally baked bread and cakes, cheeses, meat, eggs, and honey, too. Yum!

40 VISIT A PICK-YOUR-OWN FARM

Pick-your-own farms have similar environmental benefits to farmers' markets: packaging-free food and low food miles—you could even say **no** food miles if you don't count your own journey there and back! And because you pick the fruit yourself, it really is as fresh as it gets.

41 TAKE YOUR OWN SHOPPING BAGS

We all know plastic bags are bad for our planet. Not only can they end up in our oceans once they're finished with, but they use an incredible amount of fuel to produce. Plastic bags take around 1,000 years to degrade in a landfill—and even then they don't disappear completely but instead break down into tiny pieces of plastic that continue to pollute the environment.

As with many single-use plastics, if enough of us choose to stop using them, there will no longer be a need for them, and they will stop being manufactured. So be an eco-hero and take your own bags, or T-shirt tote (see page 32), with you whenever you go shopping.

HOW MANY?!
About 2 million plastic bags are used every minute worldwide. Yes, you read that right— 2 million!

CHANGE IS COMING!
Some countries, such as Kenya, in Africa, have banned selling plastic bags, and other countries now have restrictions on their use.

42 BUY FROM INDEPENDENT STORES

You need to buy a few birthday presents, a new pencil case, and a cake for Grandad—plus there's that book by your favorite author that you've had your eye on for a couple of weeks... It's time to hit the stores!

Rather than ask your grown-up to head to the main chain stores, think about whether you could get the same items from a local independent shop instead. Independent shops are usually owned and run by an individual, or family, and usually just have the one store, although they could have two or three in different locations.

You can often find items in independent shops that are made locally and aren't available in many other places, meaning there's a smaller carbon footprint and a higher chance of buying something unique as a result.

BE A HERO!

It might be tempting to resort to convenient online "one-stop-shops" to buy these kinds of things, but try to shop local instead.

43 GO SHOPPING FOR A NEIGHBOR

Next time you're heading to the store, ask whether a neighbor or friend you are due to meet up with wants anything picked up while you're there. It'll save two trips, which means fewer emissions if you both would have traveled by car. It will also feel good to help them, especially if it's an elderly neighbor living on their own.

44 VISIT THE LIBRARY

One surefire way to reduce your carbon footprint is to borrow instead of buy. It's also a great way to save money, especially if you're an avid reader!

What can be more eco-friendly than borrowing some books along the theme of conservation? See whether your local library has any of these titles on the shelves...

MY LIFE WITH THE CHIMPANZEES
JANE GOODALL

Watership Down — Richard Adams

OUR PLANET
MATT WHYMAN AND DAVID ATTENBOROUGH

The Lorax — Dr Seuss

Here We Are — Oliver Jeffers

NO ONE IS TOO SMALL TO MAKE A DIFFERENCE
GRETA THUNBERG

NOT JUST BOOKS...

As well as books, many libraries loan out other items, such as jigsaw puzzles and board games. Most libraries have computers you can use, and some host weekly or monthly events, such as sewing clubs or sessions led by local conservation groups to raise awareness of environmental issues.

45 USE THRIFT STORES

Thrift stores are fantastic! They sell good-quality clothes at a fraction of their original price, and many of them donate their profits to charity. The vast majority of items donated to thrift stores can either be reused or, failing that, recycled. This means less waste ends up in a landfill, which in turn reduces carbon emissions. When it comes to shopping, you can't get more ecological than that!

STAND OUT FROM THE CROWD

Thrift stores are a great alternative to "fast fashion" stores, which have a high carbon footprint, selling mass-produced items imported from around the world. Most of what thrift stores sell is donated, and so they are unlikely to sell two of the same item, enabling you to get your hands on some truly unique clothes!

SO MUCH VARIETY!

Thrift stores don't only sell clothes. Toys, games, books, music, household goods, dishes, furniture—all of these can be picked up in a thrift store.

GET ONLINE!

Some thrift stores now have social media accounts and web pages, so you can still support them from home.

46 GO TO A FLEA MARKET OR YARD SALE

A great way to shop sustainably is to buy from a flea market or yard sale. People gather items they don't want anymore and try to sell them, either from a flea market with lots of other sellers or, if it's a yard sale, from in front of their house.

Because anything can be sold, you never know what you might find! You could pick up some amazing bargains while also doing your bit to save the environment, as you'll be preventing items from going to a landfill.

SELL YOUR OWN ITEMS

If you have some old toys and games that you no longer need, speak to your grown-ups about organizing a yard sale. It's a great way to declutter while making a bit of money at the same time. After all, your trash could be someone else's treasure!

BE A HERO!

You could donate some of the money you make to an environmental charity.

BUDDY UP!

Gang up with a group of friends and do a joint yard sale. Make some posters to spread the word and have fun with it!

BUY SECOND-HAND ITEMS ONLINE

If you aren't able to get out and about and you have a bit of birthday or allowance money to spend, you could ask your parents to look at an online second-hand selling site with you. Everyone's heard of eBay, but there are many other selling sites you could try, including local "marketplaces" on social media.

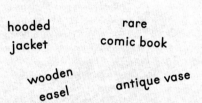

hooded jacket

rare comic book

pink sofa

wooden easel

antique vase

model car

piano

cuddly elephant

basketball hoop

wetsuit

computer games

vintage jewelry

hockey stick

skateboard

HOW TO SKATEBOARD LIKE A PRO

PICK UP A FREEBIE!

Sites such as Freecycle list things that people are willing to give away for free, to avoid unwanted —but perfectly usable—items going to a landfill. Providing the item you want is close to where you live, and therefore you don't have to make a long car journey to pick it up, it's a very planet-friendly (and pocket-friendly) way to get "new" things!

LOVE THE OUTDOORS

Pull on your walking boots, or a pair of comfy sneakers, and head out into the countryside!

48 GO ON A HIKE IN A NATIONAL PARK

There's nothing that makes you connect with nature more than feeling the sun on your skin, the breeze in your hair, and fresh air in your lungs. Pack a bag of snacks—and some sunscreen or a raincoat—and head to a national park for the day.

National parks are large areas of breathtaking natural beauty, protected against development. They may include a range of habitats such as mountains, moorlands, forests, grasslands, peat bogs, and wetlands. At most national parks, the money spent on parking or in cafés and restaurants goes back into environment and wildlife conservation work, so they really are the ultimate eco daytrip destination.

Zion National Park, Utah

VIRTUAL VISITORS

Many national parks now offer online tours. While this isn't quite the same as breathing in all the lovely fresh air yourself, it does give you the chance to explore national parks in areas you wouldn't usually be able to, like in other countries!

LOCAL PARKS

If you don't have a nationa park close by, spend a day at a local park instead. They're easier to visit for those who live in towns and cities, and you'll still enjoy the benefits of surrounding yourself with nature.

49 STAY ON TRACK!

Wherever you end up, enjoy exploring the area. But be sure to stick to pathways and tracks. Wildflowers and animal habitats all need to be protected from wandering feet. Also remember to close any gates you pass through—you don't want to accidentally allow any animals to escape!

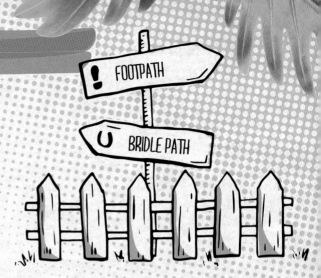

FOOTPATH

BRIDLE PATH

50 IDENTIFY WILDFLOWERS

It can be really tempting to pick a few flowers while you're out and about, and while it's generally not illegal to pick them, some species and areas are protected. So unless you know all the ins and outs of the law, it's probably best not to! Picking wildflowers can disrupt the fragile ecosystem; flowers in your backpack or pocket are no longer out there for bees and other insects to enjoy. Look, smell, touch —then sketch or photograph them instead.

KNOW YOUR CORNFLOWERS FROM YOUR COWSLIPS

Buy a flower guidebook to help you identify the blooms you spot, or download a plant identification app. Have a competition with your friends or family to see who can spot—and identify—the most!

Flowers A-Z

51 HAVE FUN WITH NATURE

Being an Earth-saving eco-hero isn't all work and no play! It's about knowing how to have fun with the world we live in, too. How many of these activities have you enjoyed? Can you check them all off?

☐ Rolling down a hill.

☐ Going fruit-picking.

☐ Climbing a tree.

☐ Playing hide-and-seek in the woods.

☐ Going fossil-hunting on a pebbly beach.

☐ Making a sculpture from rocks or pebbles.

☐ Skipping stones on a lake or by the sea.

☐ Making an obstacle course.

☐ Doing a scavenger hunt.

LOOK AND FIND!
To create a great scavenger hunt, think about the time of year and what you might find in nature. Make a list and check them off as you see them.

- [ ] Swimming in a river.

- [ ] Building a shelter in the woods.

- [ ] Creating a trail using fallen twigs as arrows.

- [ ] Getting up early to watch the sun rise.

- [ ] Going cloud-gazing and making up stories around what you see.

- [ ] Trying to identify animal tracks.

- [ ] Climbing a high hill or mountain and feeling on top of the world.

- [ ] Going geocaching and discovering hidden treasure.

- [ ] Cooking over a campfire.

SAFETY FIRST!

Fun shouldn't be dangerous. Make sure you have adult supervision when fire, water, or climbing is involved!

WHAT IS GEOCACHING?

A bit like a treasure hunt, you use GPS data on a cell phone to lead you to hidden items. It's a great way to explore your surroundings!

52 GO BIRDWATCHING

Birdwatching is a great way to learn about local wildlife and it's a fun thing to do with your family. Whether you live in a built-up inner-city area, or out in the country, there'll always be a selection of birds to spot.

Find out which birds are native to your area and create a spotting guide, or download one from the internet. There are also plenty of books that can help you identify what you see.

Some birds are very timid and won't come close, so a pair of binoculars can be useful.

ENCOURAGE THE BIRDS TO COME TO YOU
Create a bird feeder like the one on page 29, or make a bird bath out of a couple of upturned, stacked terracotta plant pots and an old ceramic plate or metal tray. Place a large stone in the middle of the plate or tray so it doesn't wobble, then fill it with water. Birds will love to bathe and drink from it!

LISTEN
As well as identifying birds by sight, find a website that features birdsong recordings to teach yourself how to recognize their calls. Your friends will be super-impressed.

53 GET BAT-FRIENDLY

Bats might be associated with horror movies and Halloween, but we needn't be scared of them. They eat bugs that can damage crops and they pollinate flowers—plus, their droppings are one of the richest fertilizers in the world. They are mini-eco-heroes in themselves!

Unfortunately, the bat population is falling due to lower insect numbers, which is because of the use of pesticides and human activity destroying their habitats. A brown bat can consume up to 1,000 insects an hour, so they need to eat plenty of bugs to keep them going!

BE A HERO!

If you have a cat, keep it indoors at night if you can. Cats don't eat bats, but they do like to play with them!

GET INVOLVED!

Find out whether there is a bat group in your area. If so, join them on a bat walk, where you can learn more about bat conservation and use a bat detector to hear the bats calling each other.

STAY SUPER!

Bats like to hunt insects in the dark, so keep outdoor lights off or turned down low.

Shhh! Everyone likes some peace and quiet from time to time, and animals are no exception. Loud noises can prevent creatures from navigating safely, and they can make it harder for them to communicate with each other when they need to warn of danger, find a mate, or challenge rivals. So think twice before cranking up those speakers. The wildlife will certainly thank you for it, as will your neighbors!

55 REPORT VANDALISM AND ILLEGAL DUMPING

Vandalism (when someone damages something on purpose) and dumping a load of trash somewhere it doesn't belong shouldn't happen, but they do. Both activities harm the environment and can be a threat to wildlife and people, especially if dangerous chemicals are present. Until humans learn that neither of these is OK, they need to be reported.

While you're out and about, if you spot acts of vandalism or illegal dumping, take a photo if possible and ask a grown-up to find out how to report it. If it's happening regularly in the same area, get in touch with your local council and see whether they can put up some signs.

Dumped trash is not only ugly, it can also be dangerous—especially if it contains harmful chemicals or toxic material.

STAY SUPER!

If you catch someone in the act, don't approach them directly. Instead, tell a grown-up what you've seen, so they can pass on the information to the appropriate authorities.

56 BE AN ECO-FRIENDLY DOG OWNER

Owning a pet might be expensive, but there are nifty ways to keep costs down. The small changes we make each day to become more environmentally friendly apply to looking after our animals, too. By choosing planet-friendly dog food and making homemade edible treats, our pooches can also be eco-heroes—without even knowing it!

BE A HERO!

If dog poop is a problem in your area, make posters to remind owners to clean up their pet's mess.

OUTSIDE!

If you have a dog, you have the best excuse to get out for a daily dose of fresh air. Dogs need plenty of exercise, and the benefits of going on regular walks are good for both you and your furry friend. Just be sure to pick up poop and dispose of it properly, and remember to keep your dog on a leash around wildlife.

IF YOU'RE MORE OF A CAT PERSON...

You can be an eco-hero-and-pet-sidekick combo, too! Put a bell on your cat's collar to help protect birds and mice, and make a cat toy by tying scraps of material to a length of string. Like dog owners, you can feed your cat environmentally friendly food and homemade treats!

HELP OUT NESTING BIRDS

Fill a traditional wire bird-feeder with fur from your pet's brush. Birds will love using it to make their nests cozy!

57 GO LITTER-PICKING

Litter. Who needs it? It looks ugly, it spreads germs, and it can be dangerous to wildlife and the environment.

Litter is any kind of trash that is dropped on the ground instead of being placed in a trash can. Plastic bags, candy wrappers, soda cans, and cigarette ends are all common pieces of litter.

YOU WILL NEED:

☑ Trash pickers (local parks often loan these out)

☑ Gloves

☑ Trash bags

REMEMBER

Never pick up sharp objects, like broken glass or syringes, with your hands.

One person really can make a difference! It doesn't take long to pick up litter, bag it, and bin it. If you have a large area to cover, organize a litter-pick with friends and have fun working together to make your surroundings beautiful again. You could do this while you enjoy a day out at a local park or at the beach.

WHY IS LITTER DANGEROUS?

Litter can attract disease-carrying rodents such as rats, be a fire hazard, or get washed down drains and end up in rivers and oceans. Litter is also really harmful to animals—they might get caught up in it or try to eat it and choke or get poisoned. Dead sea creatures and birds are often found with stomachs full of plastic, caused by discarded litter, so reducing litter can save lives.

STAY SUPER!

If you're working with friends, each person could be responsible for a different type of waste, making it easier to recycle at the end. Or you could have a competition to see who can fill their bag quickest.

Champion Collector

SPREAD THE WORD

Becoming a true eco-hero means not stopping with yourself. Use these creative suggestions in a positive and friendly way to reach out to family, friends, your school, and the local government. No voice is too small to make a big change!

SMALL CHANGES YOUR FOLKS CAN MAKE

As you've already discovered, making small changes can make a BIG difference. Now unearth your family's eco-powers by encouraging everyone else in your household to do the same!

58 SWITCH TO ENERGY-SAVING LIGHT BULBS

This is a really simple change to make. Old-fashioned filament light bulbs use lots of energy, and only 10 percent of this energy creates light—the rest is wasted heat energy! Newer LED bulbs convert nearly all the energy they use into light, which means that to create the same amount of light they use far less energy. And LED bulbs can last 10 times longer, so once your grown-ups have made the change, they can be pretty much forgotten about for quite a few years —which means less fumbling around in the dark looking for new bulbs!

59 BULK BUY

Buying in bulk means buying lots of something at the same time, and it can really help save the planet. Think about how much more packaging you'd have from two or three small boxes of your favorite cereal compared to one large box. And how many fewer supermarket trips would be required if you didn't run out of things as often. If you convince your parents to start bulk buying, you'll save them a few dollars, too. Just make sure there's room in the cupboard for the jumbo boxes of cereal first!

60 ASK ABOUT FAMILY FINANCES

No, we're not suggesting you ask how much money your nearest and dearest have—that's a very personal question. But you can find out whether they know how planet-friendly their bank is, or whether their utility providers (the companies they use for things like electricity and gas) produce their energy from carbon-free sources. If they don't know, help them find out—and suggest they switch if the answer is not good!

61 USE FSC PAPER AND WOOD

The Forest Stewardship Council is a worldwide organization that helps take care of forests and the people and wildlife that live in them. They ensure that wood is harvested in a way that is good for the environment, and that the people who work in them are treated well. So by buying FSC products you can be sure you are not contributing to the unnecessary destruction of forests and their communities.

IS IT REALLY RECYCLED?

Paper and wood showing an FSC Recycled label will have been checked to ensure it has definitely come from a recycled source. Without it, you can't be 100 percent sure!

Look for the logo!

FSC
www.fsc.org

BE A HERO!

When buying books, always make sure they show the FSC logo. The FSC Mix logo inside the cover of this book means it has been created from a mixture of recycled wood or paper, and wood that has been harvested in an eco-friendly way.

Piles of paper and cardboard are stacked up ready to be recycled at a paper mill in Italy.

62 TURN DOWN THE THERMOSTAT

It might sound a bit boring, and you've probably heard it before, but turning the household heating thermostat down can save loads of energy. Even if the temperature is set just 2°F (1°C) lower, the energy—and cost—savings across a year can be huge.

There are all kinds of nifty gadgets on the market to help your family reduce the amount of energy used for heating—from devices that learn your family's habits and adjust the thermostat accordingly, to those that automatically change the program depending on the weather forecast! You don't have to have a special device though; you can simply turn it down with your bare hands. No eco-hero superpowers required!

63 GET RID OF THE SPONGE

Typical kitchen sponges—the kind that are used to wash the dishes—are made from plastic foam and sit in a landfill for centuries. And even before they're thrown away, they release teeny-tiny bits of plastic down the drain and into the sea with each and every use.

Suggest switching to a reusable cloth cleaning pad that can be thrown in the wash, or a natural scouring pad, like those made from loofah, coconut fibers or hemp. A natural scrubber can even be put on the compost heap once you're finished with it!

Environmentally friendly dishwashing products break down naturally, keeping our rivers, lakes, and seas chemical-free.

64 WASH CLOTHES LESS...

Just because something has been worn once, it doesn't mean it has to get washed. Give it the once over and a little sniff—if it looks and smells clean, it'll last a bit longer. By washing clothes less frequently you'll save both energy and water. Your clothes will last longer and you'll also reduce the amount of micro-plastics in the sea (microscopic pieces break off synthetic garments each time they are washed). Don't be tempted to do the same with your underwear though— that really DOES need to be washed each time it's worn!

COOL IT!
Around 90 percent of the energy used to wash clothes goes towards heating the water, so wash at a lower temperature whenever you can. Avoid quick washes, too—they might sound more environmentally friendly, but in fact they often use more power, as the water has to be heated more rapidly.

65 THEN LINE DRY!

If you have outdoor space, using the power of the wind to dry clothes on a clothesline rather than an electricity-zapping dryer is a total no-brainer. It's up to you whether you offer to hang them out to dry—but you'll get in your family's good books if you do!

66 GO GREEN WHEN YOU CLEAN

OK, so you might not be the one cleaning the house, and you are even less likely to be the person actually buying all the products your home is cleaned with. But you can certainly suggest switching chemical-filled, plastic-bottled cleaners for a more ecological option to the person who does make the purchasing decisions.

Eco-friendly cleaning products reduce both water and air pollution as they don't contain nasty chemicals, and the packaging is usually plastic-free. They're kinder to your skin, too, so there's less need to wear sweaty, non-planet-friendly rubber gloves!

All of these cleaning fluids can be switched for eco versions:

- ✔ Dish soap
- ✔ Toilet cleaner
- ✔ Window cleaner
- ✔ Floor cleaner
- ✔ Disinfectant
- ✔ Multi-surface cleaner

MAKE YOUR OWN

Better still, help make some homemade cleaners using store cupboard items.

• Cut lemons are great for keeping fridges smelling fresh and tackling soap scum. Just rub them over problem areas and rinse clean.

• White vinegar mixed in equal parts with water makes a great glass cleaner. White vinegar can also be used as a fabric conditioner.

• Baking soda can do double duty as an oven cleaner. Simply mix it with a drop of water to create a paste and scrub away!

BAKING SODA

67 USE ECO-FRIENDLY TOILETRIES

When the time comes to replace your shampoo, hand soap, or toothbrush, why don't you suggest that everyone in your household makes a switch to more eco-friendly versions? Bathrooms all over the world are full of plastic bottles, containers, and tubes, but it's so easy nowadays to get hold of sustainably packaged products and reduce the amount of unnecessary waste we produce.

Besides being packaged in a more Earth-friendly way, eco-toiletries are also created with fewer chemicals, which is better for our rivers and oceans—and our skin!

Instead of using plastic disposable toothbrushes, try using bamboo ones.

Swap tubes of toothpaste for tooth soap, toothpaste tablets, or toothpaste in a glass jar.

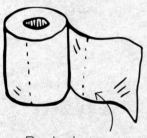

Buy bath tissue packaged in paper rather than plastic.

Bottles of hand soap can be exchanged for bars of soap.

Avoid plastic cotton buds—instead use paper ones.

Try using shampoo and conditioner bars rather than liquid in bottles.

CHANGE IS COMING!

Some toothpastes and exfoliating cleansers contain microbeads—tiny balls of plastic that can't break down. A number of countries, such as the US, the UK, and Canada, have now banned microbeads, which is a positive step towards reducing plastic waste in our oceans.

BIGGER CHANGES

Lots of small changes really add up, but there are some bigger changes your family can make, too...

68 MAKE YOUR HOME PLANET-FRIENDLY

Solar panels, double glazing, better insulation, replacing an old gas boiler... there are lots of ways your home can be altered to make it more environmentally friendly. They all work along the same lines; by reducing the amount of energy needed to heat your home.

Don't expect a quick decision from your folks on these purchases, as they can be expensive. But there are often assistance programs to help with the cost, so it might not be as pricey as everyone thinks!

BE A HERO!
All electrical appliances can be recycled. Check your local council's website for the best way to get rid of a broken item.

69 CHECK BEFORE YOU BUY

So the fridge has broken for the fifth time and your pare have decided it's finally time to get it replaced. But, befor they spend their hard-earned cash, ask them to check the new appliance's energy-efficiency rating. All electrical products are given a score on how 'green' they are; the higher the score, the better they are for the environment.

70 IF YOU NEED A NEW CAR, GO ECO!

One of the biggest causes of climate change is car pollution. Which isn't surprising when you think there are over 1 billion (1, 000, 000, 000) cars worldwide!

Vehicles that run on oil in the form of gasoline or diesel give off carbon emissions, which cause both global warming and lung-damaging air pollution. These gases also cause acid rain, which damages crops and forests. Fuel spills can seep into soil and contaminate lakes and rivers, and to top it all off, oil is nonrenewable, meaning it will run out one day. So manufacturers are inventing new ways of powering cars to help reduce harmful emissions and the amount of oil that is consumed.

An oil spill on a beach in Greece—the result of an oil tanker sinking off the coast of Athens in 2017.

ELECTRIC CARS

Electric cars are entirely battery-powered. They emit fewer greenhouse gases while traveling because they don't run on gas or diesel. Instead, they need to be plugged in for a recharge when their power runs low. In the future, as more electricity is generated from renewable sources, such as solar energy or wind power, electric cars will become a much more sustainable and eco-friendly option.

HYBRID CARS

Instead of running exclusively on electricity or oil-based fuel, hybrid cars run on a combination of the two. So they aren't as 'green' as electric cars, but they are more planet-friendly than pure gas or diesel cars.

Parking lots in many towns and cities now have charging points for electric vehicles.

CHANGE IS COMING!

Some countries, such as the UK, will soon be banning the sale of gas and diesel cars.

If your family is thinking about buying a new car, offer to help research these options and find a good solution for everyone—including the planet!

MAKE GOOD FOOD CHOICES

Our eating habits have a massive effect on the environment. Show your family how to be clever about what you buy and put on your plates—and in your mouths!

71 PLAN MEALS

You might think it's no big deal to scrape the steamed cabbage you didn't want to eat (but your parents wanted you to try!) off your plate and into the trash or compost. Or to get rid of those lovely cream donuts you nagged your folks to buy, but never ended up eating before they went bad...

But all this waste adds up. Help plan the meals for the week, so only food that will get eaten is bought. You'll probably get more of a say in what you eat, less food will go to waste, and your parents will save money. Everyone's a winner!

CLUCK!

CLUCK!

72 GO ORGANIC

Organic farming is friendlier to the environment because it uses fewer chemical pesticides and fertilizers. The chemicals used on regular crops are often made using fossil fuels and are harmful to wildlife, as they can poison insects and seep through the soil into rivers. Organically farmed animals are fed a natural diet and must be kept free-range, which means they have access to outside space.

73 CHECK THE LABELS

We all know it's better to buy free-range eggs than those from caged hens, and that we should look for toiletries that aren't tested on animals. But there are also lots of other choices you can make to ensure what you buy also helps our planet— you just need to know what information to look for!

KEEP AN EYE OUT FOR THE FOLLOWING...

Fairtrade
Fair prices are paid to farmers in developing countries so they are able to make their communities better places to live and work.

Rainforest Alliance
This means that a food or ingredient is produced in a sustainable way, protecting nature and improving the lives of farmers and their communities.

RSPO
Palm oil is a widely used vegetable oil found in nearly half of the products on sale in the supermarket! Due to its popularity, natural forests across Asia—in which many endangered species, such as orangutans and Sumatran rhinos, live—are being destroyed and replaced with palm oil trees. The Roundtable on Sustainable Palm Oil sets rules for farmers to follow, to try and make sure that palm oil is only created in a way that doesn't harm wildlife or the environment.

MSC
Standing for Marine Stewardship Council, the MSC is dedicated to ending overfishing by ensuring enough fish are left in the ocean and that habitats are not destroyed.

Dolphin safe
Often found on cans of tuna, this means the fish is caught in such a way that prevents dolphins getting caught, too.

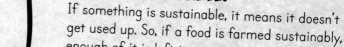

WHAT'S SUSTAINABLE?
If something is sustainable, it means it doesn't get used up. So, if a food is farmed sustainably, enough of it is left to ensure it can reproduce and continue growing in numbers.

74 EAT LESS MEAT

Global livestock farming creates as many greenhouse gases as all the world's cars, vans, and trucks put together, so eating less meat is not only good for your body, it's good for the planet! However, we're not suggesting you swap meat for potato chips and chocolate. Instead, reduce the amount of meat you eat on a day-to-day basis by including more fish, vegetables, beans, and pulses in your diet. Start with one or two days a week, and see how it goes!

STAY SUPER!

Instead of your usual café or restaurant treat, suggest visiting a vegetarian or vegan place with your family. You'll be doing your bit for the environment and you might also try some new flavors!

 # 75 USE YOUR NOSE!

"Best before" dates on food are exactly that—the date at which a product may no longer be at its best. But that doesn't mean it's not safe to eat anymore. Give it a sniff, or try a little bit first—if it seems OK, go for it!

"USE BY" DATES

"Use by" dates, on the other hand, shouldn't be ignored. These are stricter guidelines and tell you the last date a product is safe to consume. Beyond this date the food might look and smell fine, but it could contain harmful bacteria. So steer clear!

76 MAKE YOUR OWN

Fresh, homemade food always tastes better than processed food, and it's also better for you. It contains fewer preservatives, colorings, and flavorings, and often has less sugar in it. Plus, there's no extra packaging to throw away.

BE A HERO!

Smoothies are a great way to use up fruit that's starting to go a bit squishy and would likely end up in the trash!

SUPER SMOOTHIE

Try this smoothie recipe and create a healthy drink that tantalizes your taste buds more than anything you get in a bottle or carton!

You will need:

- A handful of fresh or frozen fruit—berries, bananas, and other soft fruit work best
- A few dollops of plain yogurt
- A splash of milk (dairy or non-dairy, it's up to you)
- A blender or food processor, and a glass

Simply whizz up all the ingredients in your blender or food processor before pouring them into your glass. If your smoothie is too thick, add some extra milk, and if you'd like it sweeter, stir in a little honey.

It's best to drink your smoothie as soon as you make it, but you can keep it in the fridge for a day or so. Just be aware that the fruit might start to discolor the longer you leave it.

If you like a thick smoothie, use less milk.

HOW ABOUT SOME OTHER IDEAS?

Pasta sauces, soups, and pizzas are all really easy to make yourself, and they're great for using up bits and pieces in the fridge. Ask a grown-up if you can search for some recipes online.

77 USE UP OLD INGREDIENTS

While smoothies are a great way to use up old fruit, what do you do with other food items that need eating up? Savory leftovers can often be used as sandwich or wrap fillings, pasta ingredients, or pizza toppings—use your imagination and get creative in the kitchen!

Another good way to use up food in the fridge that will soon go out of date is to find a recipe online. Simply type the names of the ingredients you need to use up followed by "recipe" into a search engine and discover a whole host of meals to choose from. You never know, you might discover a new favorite dish!

BE A HERO!

Sometimes, old ingredients can be better than fresh ones! Over-ripe bananas are great for banana bread, and squishy-but-still-safe-to-eat soft fruit like peaches and strawberries make yummy jam.

78 FREEZE!

You've been invited to lunch by your great aunt, and she's made enough of her delicious bean chili to feed your entire school! Rather than trying to squeeze in a third bowlful, suggest she freezes what's left in the pan for another day. Freezing leftovers is a great way to both reduce waste and reduce the number of shopping trips you (or your elderly relatives) have to make.

GET THE BIG PANS OUT!

Cooking double - or even triple - the amount of something in order to save some for another day is called batch cooking. Just ask the person who plans the meals to buy extra ingredients—and you could also halve the work if you help them cook it!

79 DONATE TO A FOOD BANK

Food banks are a bit like grocery stores, but everything is free. If your family is struggling and in need of food and everyday essentials such as bath tissue and dish soap, you can visit a food bank. Or, if you think you might have anything spare or surplus to requirement at home, you and your grown-ups can have a rummage in your kitchen cupboards and donate items to your local food bank the next time you're passing by. It's also a nice idea to buy a couple of extra items from the supermarket to donate when you can, if your family can afford to.

What can I donate?

Most groceries with a long shelf life can be donated to a food bank. Here are some suggestions:

- Rice or dried pasta
- Cereal
- Canned fruit and vegetables, soup, and fish / meat
- Jarred food like pasta sauce
- Lentils, beans, and pulses
- Cookies
- Tea and coffee
- UHT milk
- Pet food
- Dish soap
- Laundry detergent
- Toiletries, such as deodorant, soap, and toothpaste
- Diapers

STAY SUPER!

Your local food bank will often have an up-to-date list explaining what kinds of things they are low on. So, if you're thinking of donating, check with them first to see what they need.

Check that whatever you're donating is well within its sell by date.

VOLUNTEER!

Helping a local conservation cause will not only benefit the environment and your community, it will also have a positive impact on your own well-being. Join in and feel good!

80 LEND A HELPING HAND

Being a volunteer is about giving up your time to help out without getting paid for it. It's a great way for you and your family and friends to get involved and make a real difference to your community.

Many local charities have opportunities for family volunteering. Search online to see what's going on in your area. You might find a nature reserve looking for volunteers to count the number of butterflies they spot, a community garden that needs help with weeding, planting, or watering, or a park looking for some extra pairs of hands to help clear a pathway or build a fence. Have fun learning new skills and sharing experiences while knowing you are doing something positive to help the environment.

Volunteering is good for you, too!

- ☑ See your own actions make a real difference.
- ☑ Make new friends.
- ☑ Have fun learning new skills.
- ☑ Improve your mood and reduce stress and anxiety by being outside.
- ☑ Keep active, which is good for your body.
- ☑ Help others, which in turn makes you feel happier and healthier.

THINKING AHEAD

You might not know what career you want when you're older, but if you have a feeling that you'd like to be involved in conservation, then volunteering is a fantastic way to gain some experience and find out what it's all about.

BE A HERO!

There are other ways to help eco-charities without volunteering your time. For example, you could become a member of an international conservation group, although there's often a small monthly fee. See pages 98–99 for ideas of groups you could support.

TAKE A FAMILY ECO-BREAK

Even eco-heroes need some time out.
But you don't have to hang up your
cape and mask while you're away...

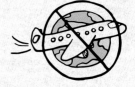

81 VACATION LOCALLY

Most forms of transportation contribute to climate change, but airplanes are one of the worst. It takes an unbelievable amount of fuel to get a plane up into the air, and the noise pollution is an additional downside of air travel.

But if giving up your overseas holiday is an eco-step too far, then there are ways to make your trip more planet-friendly. Flying with an economy airline means more passengers per plane, resulting in a smaller carbon footprint per person. Packing fewer clothes in your suitcase makes it lighter, so less fuel is needed to fly the plane. And using an airline or travel company that offsets the carbon emissions of your flight by investing in ecological projects, such as rainforest management and clean water schemes, helps, too.

82 BUY ETHICAL SOUVENIRS

Spending your vacation money on trinkets to take home is part of the fun of going away, and buying ethically sourced souvenirs is a really important way to help benefit the local people. Be wary of typical tourist shops; they are likely to be full of mass-produced gifts that are made cheaply and imported from overseas. It's better to spend your currency at farmers' markets or traditional craft stalls, as they are more likely to sell genuine, local goods. If you're looking for an authentic souvenir, avoid items that claim to be "Made in China"— unless, of course, you ARE in China!

83 TAKE A CONSERVATION TRIP

If you'd like a family break with a difference, why not try a volunteering vacation? You'll learn new things while having the satisfaction of knowing you are doing something positive to help our planet. Whether you choose a base close to home or an overseas adventure, there are plenty of options for a hands-on, helping holiday. And if you travel to a different country, you'll also get to experience other cultures and traditions in a way you'd never be able to on a "normal" vacation.

Which trip would you choose?

Planting banana trees in Thailand.

Helping orphaned kangaroos at a sanctuary in Australia.

Protecting nesting turtles in Costa Rica.

Restoring the native forests of Hawaii.

Elephant conservation work in Sri Lanka.

Working on an organic farm in rural France.

Monitoring bat species in Scotland, UK.

Coastline cleaning in Iceland.

Rehabilitating horses in South Africa.

Installing clean water pumps in Mali, Africa.

84 GO CAMPING

If you love the outdoors and being surrounded by nature, then there's no better family vacation than one under canvas! But even the most enthusiastic eco-hero can find it tricky to stay green when away from home. Here are some tips that might help you and your folks plan a perfectly planet-friendly camping trip.

CAMP OFF-GRID

This means camping without electricity. It might seem scary, but how much electricity do you REALLY need when out in the wild? You can always pack a portable charger to keep a cell phone topped up for emergencies.

ENJOY A CAMPFIRE MEAL

Gas stoves are convenient, but they give off harmful chemicals. Cooking on an actual fire, made from kindling (small dried sticks) you've gathered from the ground, is much more fun! Plus, it's better for the planet, as long as you are super-careful not to damage the local environment in the process. However, if you're camping in a hot country, avoid lighting fires in the summer months—there is the danger you might start a wildfire.

Never light a fire without checking first that the campsite you're staying at allows them.

PACK WISELY

No batteries required

Rather than a battery-powered flashlight, take a wind-up one for those night-time bathroom trips and spooky campfire stories.

Keep clean the chemical-free way

Make sure you pack your eco-toiletries (see page 79). Campsites often have simple plumbing systems, and sometimes pipes from sinks run directly into the land you're camping on, so try to avoid using dish soaps, soaps, and shampoos full of chemicals.

Cool it!

A cooler and some freezer blocks should keep your food chilled for a couple of days. Some campsites have freezers you can keep blocks in as well, so take a few spare and rotate them.

SAFETY FIRST!

Always make sure you are with a responsible grown-up if you are lighting a fire.

LEAVE NO TRACE

Make sure you take all your trash home with you, and restore the area to how it was when you arrived. It should look like you've never even been there. What camping trip?!

93

GET FRIENDS INVOLVED

If one eco-hero alone can make a difference,
just imagine what a group of eco-heroes can achieve!
Invite your friends over and have some fun while you fix the world.

85 HOST A MOVIE NIGHT – WITH A DIFFERENCE!

Who doesn't love a movie night? Invite your friends over to watch an eco-documentary or a film with an environmental twist and feel inspired. Here are some great films, all with an ecological message, for you to try...

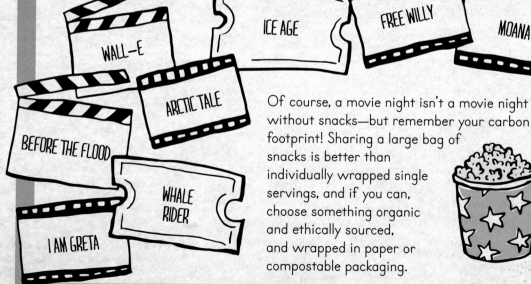

HAPPY FEET

THE LORAX

ICE AGE

FREE WILLY

MOANA

WALL-E

ARCTIC TALE

BEFORE THE FLOOD

WHALE RIDER

I AM GRETA

Of course, a movie night isn't a movie night without snacks—but remember your carbon footprint! Sharing a large bag of snacks is better than individually wrapped single servings, and if you can, choose something organic and ethically sourced, and wrapped in paper or compostable packaging.

86 ORGANIZE AN OUTDOOR GAMES NIGHT

If the weather's being kind to you, put the movie night on hold and organize some outdoor group games instead. You'll be saving electricity and enjoying yourselves at the same time.

THREE-LEGGED RACES

HIDE AND SEEK

CAPTURE THE FLAG

TUG OF WAR

TAG

DODGEBALL

87 STARGAZE!

Take your focus away from your own planet for the evening and marvel at the universe beyond. Studying the night sky really makes you recognize how precious and unique life on Earth is.

Super stargazing tips:

* Ask your grown-ups to help you choose a spot away from city lights for the clearest view.

* There's no point in trying to stargaze if it's cloudy. Just do it another night!

* Take a blanket so you can lie down and not strain your neck.

* Allow your eyes time to get used to the dark. You will see much more after about 20–30 minutes, once your eyes have adjusted to low-light conditions.

* Check what you see against a constellation book, or download an app that allows you to hold your phone up to the night sky and plot the stars, planets, and satellites.

88 HOST A SWAP MEET

Swapping and sharing is a fantastic alternative to buying new and it saves loads of stuff from going to a landfill. Get together with your friends and have a fun-filled afternoon without spending a cent!

Best for bookworms

A book swap is easy to organize. Just ask a few friends to bring some books and magazines they have already read and are happy to see go to a new home. You could even get your school on board and make it a mega-swap!

Best for green-fingered pals

If you like to grow fruit and vegetables from seed, you may well end up with too many, so why not share your plants —and tips on how to grow them—with your pals? This swap meet is probably best to organize outside, in a garden, where it doesn't matter if a bit of soil gets spilled.

PLAN AHEAD

Decide in advance what to do with the leftover items. Thrift stores will take clothes and books, and you could donate plants to a community garden or school—or just leave them outside your house with a "Help Yourself" sign!

Best for friends of the same age

A clothes swap is an entertaining and easy way for you and your buddies to update your wardrobes! Put on some music, create a pile of clothes each of you no longer wants in the middle of the room, and dive right in! Just make sure you have areas for your friends to get changed and a full-length mirror handy.

89 CREATE A SELF-PORTRAIT FROM JUNK

An empty cereal box for a head, an old plastic bottle as a nose, and shredded paper for hair—what crazy creations can you and your friends make from trash destined for the recycling bin?

Set yourselves a junk-modeling challenge and see how creative you can get!

You can use all kinds of trash. Just make sure everything is clean and safe before you start!

You will need:
• A selection of items heading for the trash—food packaging trays, plastic bottles, lids, cardboard tubes, boxes, egg cartons, paper, candy wrappers —anything goes!
• Scissors
• Glue
• Sticky tape
• Decorations such as old buttons, thread, fabric scraps, paint, etc.

FUNDRAISING

Many environmental charities and conservation groups rely on fundraising to help them continue their good work. Find an eco-organization you would like to support, then try one of these ideas to help them raise some much-needed cash.

90 GET SPONSORED

Be sure your challenge is an eco-friendly one!

Getting sponsored to do something is a great way to raise funds for a cause you support, and the bonus is you can make it as hard, or as imaginative, as you like. The idea is that you set yourself a challenge and ask for donations from friends and families to complete it.

You could choose to walk, run, or cycle a certain distance each day for a month, swim laps at a local pool, read lots of books, or learn to spell some tricky words. It has to be a challenge; rather than trying to get sponsored for eating candy each day, a sponsored silence might make your charity lots of money!

Who can I help?
You could support one of these international organizations. They all work in some way towards making our planet a better place. Or do some research and find another charity.

 The **World Wide Fund for Nature (WWF)** is the world's largest conservation organization. It aims to protect communities, wildlife, and the places in which they live. **https://wwf.panda.org**

 Friends of the Earth seeks to protect the natural world by reducing climate change. **https://foe.org**

91 MAKE SOMETHING AND SELL IT

1.50

an you bake cupcakes, make lemonade, or create
iendship bracelets? If so, host a sale and raise money
r your cause. Create posters to advertise the event,
ating clearly that you are raising money for
environmental charity and why it's
portant to you.

92 DONATE SOME OF YOUR ALLOWANCE

ch time you receive some money,
u could put a bit aside to donate.
ep a separate jar dedicated to your
arity so it's easier to manage. You
uld even ask for donations instead
presents for your birthday or
ristmas from a couple of people—
u probably won't even notice that
u have fewer gifts!

Tips for a great sale:

• Ask some friends or grown-ups to help you organize your event.
• Create signs for the different things you are selling and make sure everything is clearly priced.

• Make sure you have plenty of coins you can give as change.

• Colorful decorations and an eye-catching display will help attract customers.

• You are raising money for an environmental cause, so make sure that your products are eco-friendly!

• If you are selling something that might generate waste, make sure you have a trash can handy.

Greenpeace is another cause working towards protection and conservation of the environment.
https://www.greenpeace.org/usa

Environmental Defense Fund is working towards a safer and healthier environment, guided by science. **edf.org**

Rainforest Action Network helps preserve rainforests and the communities that live within them. **ran.org**

SPREAD THE WORD AT SCHOOL

School is a place to share ideas and learn from others. And it's full of future planet-savers! Get your teachers and classmates on board and you'll have a whole school full of eco-heroes in no time!

93 THE THREE R'S AT SCHOOL: REDUCE, REUSE, AND RECYCLE

REDUCE PAPER WASTE

Do you need to print everything you do on the school computer? Can you hand your homework in online? And rather than start a new page in your class notebook, could you draw a line under the previous activity and carry on underneath instead? Thinking about ways to reduce waste in school is just as important as it is at home. Plus, if you're using less paper, you'll save your school money, too, which means they'll have more they can set aside for school trips and new technology.

REUSE WHAT YOU CAN

At the start of the new school year, instead of asking your grown-ups for a shiny new pencil case, lunch box, and backpack, look at what you already have. Do you really need to replace everything or can you reuse some of it? Lots of school supplies are made from plastic, or packaged in it—and things might not even need replacing in the first place, especially if you've looked after them!

STAY SUPER!

Be sure to write your name on all your belongings, so that if you lose them you're more likely to get them back —and less likely to have to go and buy something new.

SET UP A RECYCLING HUB

Things like old felt tip pens, potato chip packets, ink cartridges, and coffee pods can all be recycled, but unfortunately many local councils don't include them as part of their regular waste collection. But this doesn't mean they should end up in a landfill! Ask your principal to set up a recycling point at school. Once you are all set up and ready to accept donations, let your local community know that they can come to you to recycle some of their waste.

BE A HERO!

You might recycle like a pro at home, but how about at school? If your classroom doesn't have separate recycling bins, ask your teacher if they can be provided.

POTATO CHIPS

94 START A CLUB

If you like hanging out with your eco-mates at lunchtime, be proactive and ask a teacher whether you can set up an environmentally themed club to get children from other classes involved. It could be something specific like a gardening club to grow fruit, vegetables, and flowering plants for pollinators or a nature club in which you can create a bug hotel or do some birdwatching. Or it could simply be a more general eco-club where you all just get together to share ideas on how best to save the planet.

95 SUGGEST AN ECO-TRIP

Who doesn't love a school trip? Nature reserves, outdoor education centers, natural history museums, and even your local landfill site or recycling center are all really cool places to visit with your classmates. Ask at school whether your next outing can have an ecological theme, and suggest some places to your teacher if he or she is looking for inspiration.

96 CREATE POSTERS FOR YOUR CLASSROOM

Get creative and design some bright, eye-catching posters to help persuade your friends and teachers to be more eco. You could use them to remind people to shut doors, turn off lights and taps, or recycle their paper. Ask each class to create their own, or turn it into a whole-school competition with some kind of reward or treat from the principal for the best ones.

SWITCH OFF AND SAVE ENERGY!

97 SET UP A WALKING BUS

Despite its name, a walking bus isn't a bus with legs; it's a group of children walking to school with one or more adults. A walking bus helps the environment because fewer cars travel on the streets around your school as a result, meaning less congestion and less pollution. It also improves road safety for these reasons, too.

You'll have to get a few parents and carers involved to help you plan a route, and there'll need to be a rota so everyone can take turns to supervise. But once you have grown-up help, it'll be easy to get the scheme up and running—or walking!

If a walking bus won't work in your community, then cycling and scooting to school are also good ecological alternatives to taking the car. Or, for those families who don't live close enough to walk, cycle, or scoot, your teachers could suggest a carpooling scheme where families take turns to take each other's children to school.

BE A HERO!

If your school doesn't already have equipment such as bike or scooter racks, ask your principal if they can order some.

SHARE THE MESSAGE!

Be inspired by real-life eco-heroes like Greta Thunberg and make your voice heard in whichever way you can.

98 CONTACT LOCAL GOVERNMENT OFFICIALS

Your local council might need a helping hand in making your community greener. You can get in touch with them and explain your concerns about climate change and what could be changed locally to help fight it. You could also contact your local government representative, whose job is to give the people in the local area a voice in the government. Find out what environmental policies your representative supports online, and what differences they are trying to make. Then send a letter or e-mail thanking them for what they are already doing and giving your own suggestions on how to save the planet.

GRETA THE GREAT

Born in 2003, Swedish environmental and eco-superhero activist Greta Thunberg has been standing up for the planet since she was young, helping to raise awareness of issues surrounding climate change.

99 WRITE TO THE LOCAL PRESS

Writing a letter or e-mail to the editor of your local newspaper or community magazine is the perfect way to get your views out there. You may even inspire the editor to write a full article about the topic, or even get asked to write an article yourself! The great thing about getting your thoughts published, whether in print or online, is that you never know who could be reading them—and you could see some real change as a result!

100 START A PETITION

A petition is a document asking for change, and people sign their names to show they support it. Petitions can have a real impact, as they raise awareness about a cause and get people talking about it.

Petitions can be about pretty much anything. Here are some ideas to get you started:
• Ask your principal to include recycling bins in each classroom, or to reduce plastic waste in the cafeteria.
• Send a petition to your local government representative asking for more bike lanes on the roads around your school.
• Request fast-food restaurants stop using plastic straws, cutlery, and sauce sachets.
• Petition your government to ban the sale of bee-killing pesticides.

101 SPEAK UP!

One of the biggest ways you can make a change is through your voice. Every time you make an eco-friendly choice, you are making a statement and educating others. Continue to explain why you are doing the things you do, and you are very likely to influence and inspire others to do the same.

Once everyone starts realizing how precious Earth is, we can all work together to protect it. By making changes to the way we live, eco-heroes—just like you —will win the battle against climate change and save the future of our planet!

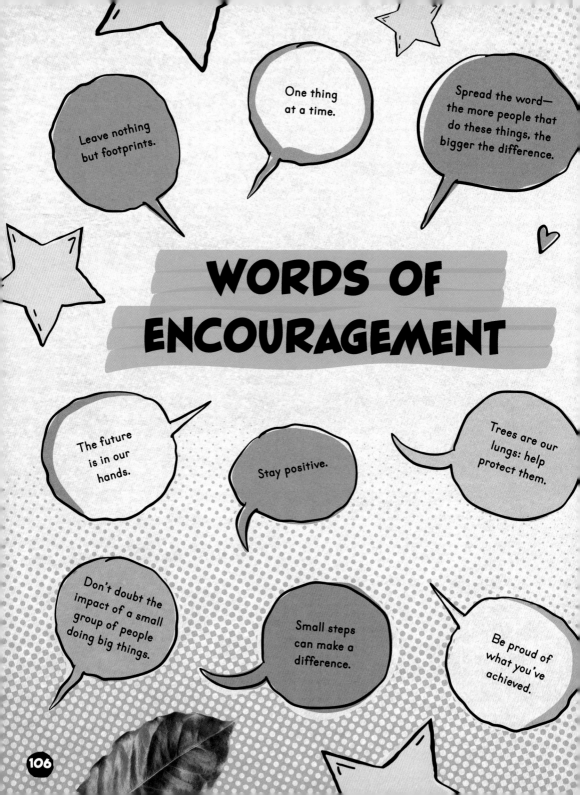

WORDS OF ENCOURAGEMENT

I AM AN ECO-HERO!

Here's a checklist of all 101 ways you can make a difference. Check each one off as you complete it.

P.8 SAVING THE PLANET BEGINS AT HOME

- [ ] #1 Check your carbon footprint
- [ ] #2 Shower instead of bath
- [ ] #3 Turn off lights and electronics
- [ ] #4 Turn off the tap
- [ ] #5 Shut that door!
- [ ] #6 Make the most of paper
- [ ] #7 Make a "No Junk Mail" sign
- [ ] #8 Create a homemade scrapbook
- [ ] #9 Turn off your screens!
- [ ] #10 Recycling vs. landfill
- [ ] #11 If it's broken, fix it!
- [ ] #12 Recycling electronics
- [ ] #13 From trash to treasure
- [ ] #14 Avoid single-use plastic
- [ ] #15 Give up the gum!
- [ ] #16 Host a plastic-free party!
- [ ] #17 Give non-plastic presents
- [ ] #18 Plastic bottle crafts
- [ ] #19 Revamp old clothes
- [ ] #20 Create a costume
- [ ] #21 Make a T-shirt tote bag
- [ ] #22 Donate
- [ ] #23 Plant plants for pollinators
- [ ] #24 Help a bee in need
- [ ] #25 Create a mini-pond
- [ ] #26 Make a bug hotel
- [ ] #27 Grow your own

- [ ] #28 Composting
- [ ] #29 Make plant food
- [ ] #30 Recycle rainwater

P.42. OUT AND ABOUT

- [ ] #31 Take a public transit road trip
- [ ] #32 Discover places on your doorst
- [ ] #33 Ditch the car
- [ ] #34 Go on a bike ride
- [ ] #35 Go kayaking, canoeing, or paddle-boarding
- [ ] #36 Go surfing or bodyboarding
- [ ] #37 Have a litter-free picnic
- [ ] #38 Eat out responsibly
- [ ] #39 Go to a farmers' market
- [ ] #40 Visit a pick-your-own farm
- [ ] #41 Take your own shopping bags
- [ ] #42 Buy from independent shops
- [ ] #43 Go shopping for a neighbor
- [ ] #44 Visit the library
- [ ] #45 Use thrift stores
- [ ] #46 Go to a flea market or yard sa
- [ ] #47 Buy second-hand items online
- [ ] #48 Go on a hike at a national park
- [ ] #49 Stay on track!
- [ ] #50 Identify wildflowers
- [ ] #51 Have fun with nature
- [ ] #52 Go birdwatching

- ☐ **#53** Get bat-friendly
- ☐ **#54** Help cut noise pollution
- ☐ **#55** Report vandalism and illegal dumping
- ☐ **#56** Be an eco-friendly dog owner
- ☐ **#57** Go litter-picking

P72 SPREAD THE WORD

- ☐ **#58** Switch to energy-saving light bulbs
- ☐ **#59** Bulk buy
- ☐ **#60** Ask about family finances
- ☐ **#61** Use FSC paper and wood
- ☐ **#62** Turn down the thermostat
- ☐ **#63** Get rid of the sponge
- ☐ **#64** Wash clothes less...
- ☐ **#65** Then line dry!
- ☐ **#66** Go green when you clean
- ☐ **#67** Use eco-friendly toiletries
- ☐ **#68** Make your home planet-friendly
- ☐ **#69** Check before you buy
- ☐ **#70** If you need a new car, go eco!
- ☐ **#71** Plan meals
- ☐ **#72** Go organic
- ☐ **#73** Check the labels
- ☐ **#74** Eat less meat
- ☐ **#75** Use your nose!
- ☐ **#76** Make your own
- ☐ **#77** Use up old ingredients
- ☐ **#78** Freeze!

- ☐ **#79** Donate to a food bank
- ☐ **#80** Lend a helping hand
- ☐ **#81** Vacation locally
- ☐ **#82** Buy ethical souvenirs
- ☐ **#83** Take a conservation trip
- ☐ **#84** Go camping
- ☐ **#85** Host a movie night— with a difference!
- ☐ **#86** Organize an outdoor games night
- ☐ **#87** Stargaze!
- ☐ **#88** Host a swap meet
- ☐ **#89** Create a self-portrait from junk
- ☐ **#90** Get sponsored
- ☐ **#91** Make something and sell it
- ☐ **#92** Donate some of your allowance
- ☐ **#93** The three R's at school: reduce, reuse, and recycle
- ☐ **#94** Start a club
- ☐ **#95** Suggest an eco-trip
- ☐ **#96** Create posters for your classroom
- ☐ **#97** Set up a walking bus
- ☐ **#98** Contact local government officials
- ☐ **#99** Write to the local press
- ☐ **#100** Start a petition
- ☐ **#101** Speak up!

FIND OUT MORE

NASA: CLIMATE KIDS
www.climatekids.nasa.gov
Interactive and informative activities, games and resources that teach you about the Earth's systems so that you can better understand the impact climate change has on our natural environment.

NO ONE IS TOO SMALL TO MAKE A DIFFERENCE
by Greta Thunberg
(Allen Lane, 2019)
An illustrated edition of the impact of Greta Thunberg's activism, including her speeches and images of her climate-tackling journey, and the movement she has started.

ECO KIDS PLANET
www.ecokidsplanet.co.uk
A magazine full of colorful, educational content surrounding all things nature.

WILD CHILD: A JOURNEY THROUGH NATURE
Dara McAnulty
(Macmillan Children's Books, 2021)
A handbook for young conservationists about the joy of nature, by the author of *Diary of a Young Naturalist*.
Learn how to craft and explore your own eco-wilderness, from building a terrarium to planting wildflowers.

GREENPEACE EDUCATION RESOURCES FOR YOUNG PEOPLE
www.greenpeace.org.uk/all-resources/education-resources
A selection of different resources for you, your family and school to explore the ways in which we can take eco action, whether at home, in local communities or out in the natural world.

CHARLIE AND LOLA LOOK AFTER YOUR PLANET
by Lauren Child
(Puffin Books, 2011)
A funny, playful look at the ways in which we can start recycling at home.